MW01228764

Come, Follow Me
Lessons & Activities
FOR CHILDREN & FAMILIES

Gather your family and get ready to teach fun & engaging gospel lessons that your kids will love! Dive into the Doctrine and Covenants and discover how consistent Come, Follow Me lessons will strengthen your family.

In the following pages, you will find a variety of countless, age-appropriate activities, hand-drawn materials and lesson plans for your children that include all the details, descriptions and supply lists you will need to make Come, Follow Me easy and meaningful.

Follow us!

 @ comefollowmefhe

 facebook.com/comefollowmefhe

 pinterest.com/comefollowmefhe

comefollowmefhe.com

Table of Contents

"The Worth of Souls is Great"

February 24-March 2
Doctrine & Covenants 18

Supplies

crayons, colored pencils old or new T-shirts
scissors Sharpies or fabric markers
1 die

 ### Scripture Study

Help your family learn about Oliver Cowdery and David Whitmer searching out the 12 Apostles as you read D&C 18:26-36. Jump from one **"stepping stone"** to another as you read each verse out loud. At the end of all the verses, you will reach the picture of the year 1835 Quorum of the 12 Apostles. Share your testimony of the Lord's Apostles and things you have learned from them. (pg. 4-26)

 ### Go & Do Activity

In D&C 18: 15-16, 44 we are told that sharing the gospel of Jesus Christ can bring joy! Watch a message from Pres. Nelson where he invites the youth to experience the joy of missionary service. As a family, think of some ways you can joyfully share the gospel. See our **Go & Do page** for details. (pg. 27)

 ### Hands-on Activity

Read D&C 18:35-36 with your family. Discuss how we can have the words of God that He reveals to our prophet. Play the **Follow The North Star board game**. Discuss how just like the North Star can guide us, we have been given a prophet and apostles to be our "North Star." If we follow them we will always find our way back to Heavenly Father. (pg. 28-34)

 ### Media Page

This week, you get to watch three videos:
1. Sharing Your Beliefs,
2. The Starfish Story and
3. Elder Patrick Kearon called to the Quorum of the Twelve Apostles. Plus, you'll also learn these three songs: 1. My Heavenly Father Loves Me, 2. Come with Me to Primary and
3. We'll Bring the World His Truth. See our **media page** to enjoy these as a family. (pg. 35)

 ### Surprise Activity

Have fun making **"#1 Fan" T-shirts** with your family. Each person will make a shirt to cheer on another family member. After making your T-shirts read D&C 18:10. Explain that Heavenly Father loves all of His children and we are of great worth to Him. He is your #1 fan! It's good to celebrate and remind each other that we have worth. See the instruction page for details. (pg. 36)

 ### Coloring Page

Read D&C 18:35-36 and explain how following the North Star for directions is like following the prophet and apostles for guidance on how to return to our Heavenly Father. Color the **North Star coloring page** as you talk together. (pg. 37-38)

*Grab your paper, pencil and coloring supplies to have fun with our Scripture Sketches videos!
This month's video is "Souls of Great Worth." Find the video in your account.

*Remember, subscribers always get 40% off digital products in our shop and free shipping on any physical products!

comefollowmefhe.com

5 WAYS TO USE OUR
MEDIA PAGE

1. Print & Present
Purchase a clear picture frame. Then, print the media pages two weeks at a time, double-sided. Slide the pages into the frame and display them where they will be easily seen, like the kitchen table for dinnertime devotionals or the breakfast nook for meaningful morning moments.

2. Scan & Show
Login to your account on our website mobily, then select the Elementary Bundle for this week and find the media page inside. Click on the titles of the videos to show your family. Be sure to read the scriptures that goes along with it.

3. Teens & Teaching
Print the media page each week and hand it to your teen. Let them read the short paragraph and scripture about each video and then pre-watch the video. Assign them a night of the week to teach the family!

4. Church & Children
Use the media page in your calling. Whether you are a Primary, Youth Sunday School or Young Mens/Womens teacher, this is a great resource in our Elementary Bundle that works for every age!

5. Individual & Important
Enjoy our media page for your personal study. It's easy to access on your phone first thing in the morning or before bed to create a quiet moment reflecting and learning about what is most important! Record your thoughts and impressions that come to your mind! Don't love doing personal study on a device? Simply print the media pages for the whole month and keep them on your bedside table to watch the inspired messages as you need them throughout the week.

Acrylic Frames

WHERE TO FIND OUR
SKETCH THE SCRIPTURES
VIDEOS

1. Go to our website: comefollowmefhe.com.
2. Click Login in the top right corner.
3. Login with your username and password.
4. Click on "Access Member Area" in the "My Membership" box.
5. Click on the "Sketch the Scriptures Videos" tab.
6. Now have fun drawing with your family!

Scripture Stepping Stones

1835 Quorum
of 12 Apostles

You'll need to prep a few things for this beforehand:
1. Print the stepping stones and picture of the 12 Apostles in 1835 (click/scan QR code).
2. Clear a space in your home so you can have room to jump from stepping stone to stepping stone.
3. Place the stepping stone pictures on the floor, in a line and in order with the 12 Apostles picture at the end of the line.

Start by explaining the scriptures you are going to read. Oliver Cowdery and David Whitmer are being told to find the 12 people who are to be called as the 12 Apostles of the Lord's church. These verses tell them what to look for in these 12 people.

Tell your family that you will read the verses out loud, then pause after each one so they can read (or you can read it to them) the stepping stone and then jump to the stepping stone. Then you will read the next verse and continue until you reach the end of verse 36, where there will be a picture of the Quorum of the 12 Apostles in 1835, the men David Whitmer and Oliver Cowdery found after receiving this revelation.

Doctrine and Covenants 18:26-36
26: Declare My Gospel
27: My Name
28: Go Into all the World
29: Ordained
30: Words
31: Walk Uprightly
32: Holy Ghost
33: Jesus Christ
34: Testify
35: Spirit
36: Testify

After your reading, share your testimony of the Lord's apostles and what you have learned from them.

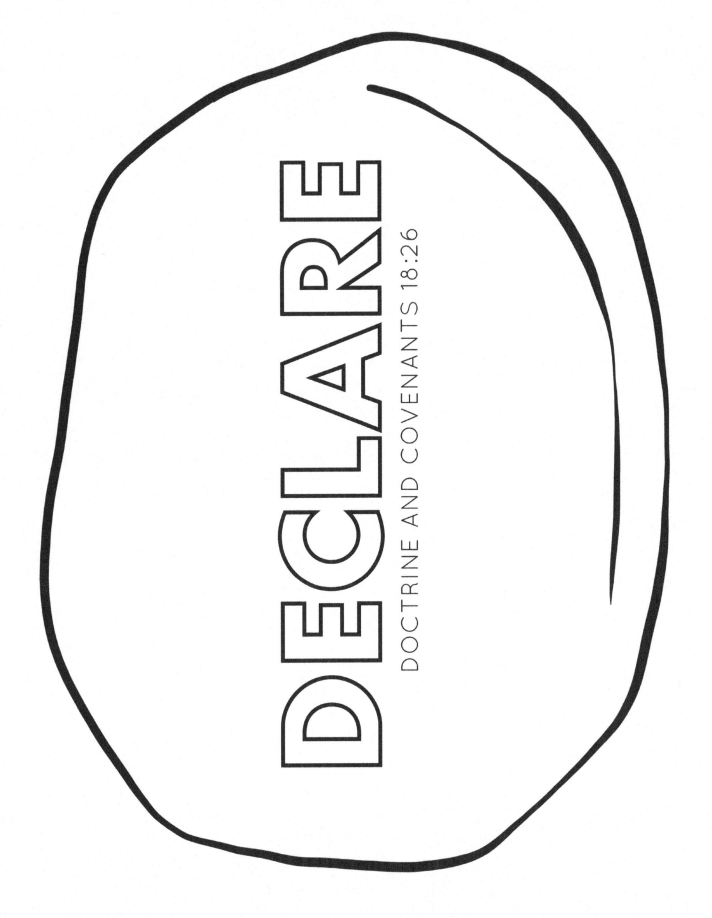

DECLARE

DOCTRINE AND COVENANTS 18:26

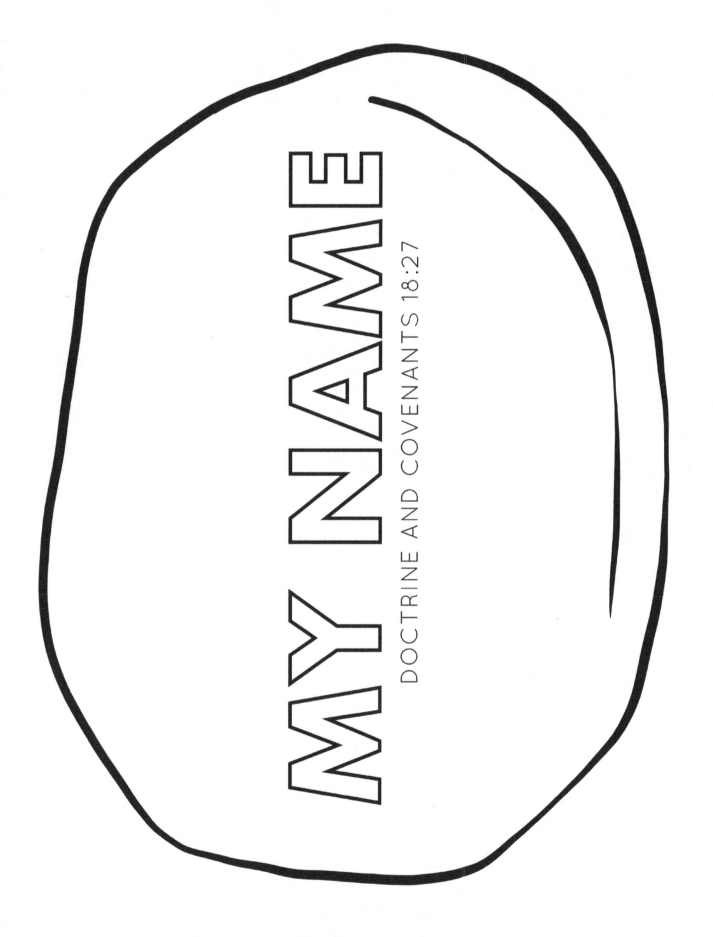

MY NAME

DOCTRINE AND COVENANTS 18:27

ALL THE WORLD

DOCTRINE AND COVENANTS 18:28

ORDAINED

DOCTRINE AND COVENANTS 18:29

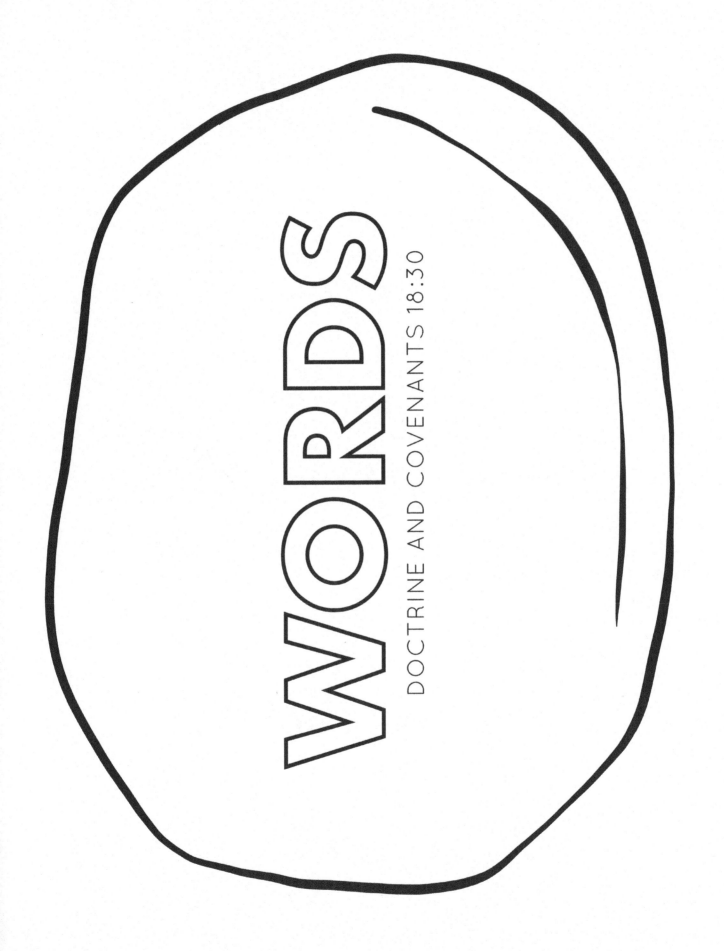

WORDS

DOCTRINE AND COVENANTS 18:30

WALK UPRIGHTLY

DOCTRINE AND COVENANTS 18:31

HOLY GHOST

DOCTRINE AND COVENANTS 18:32

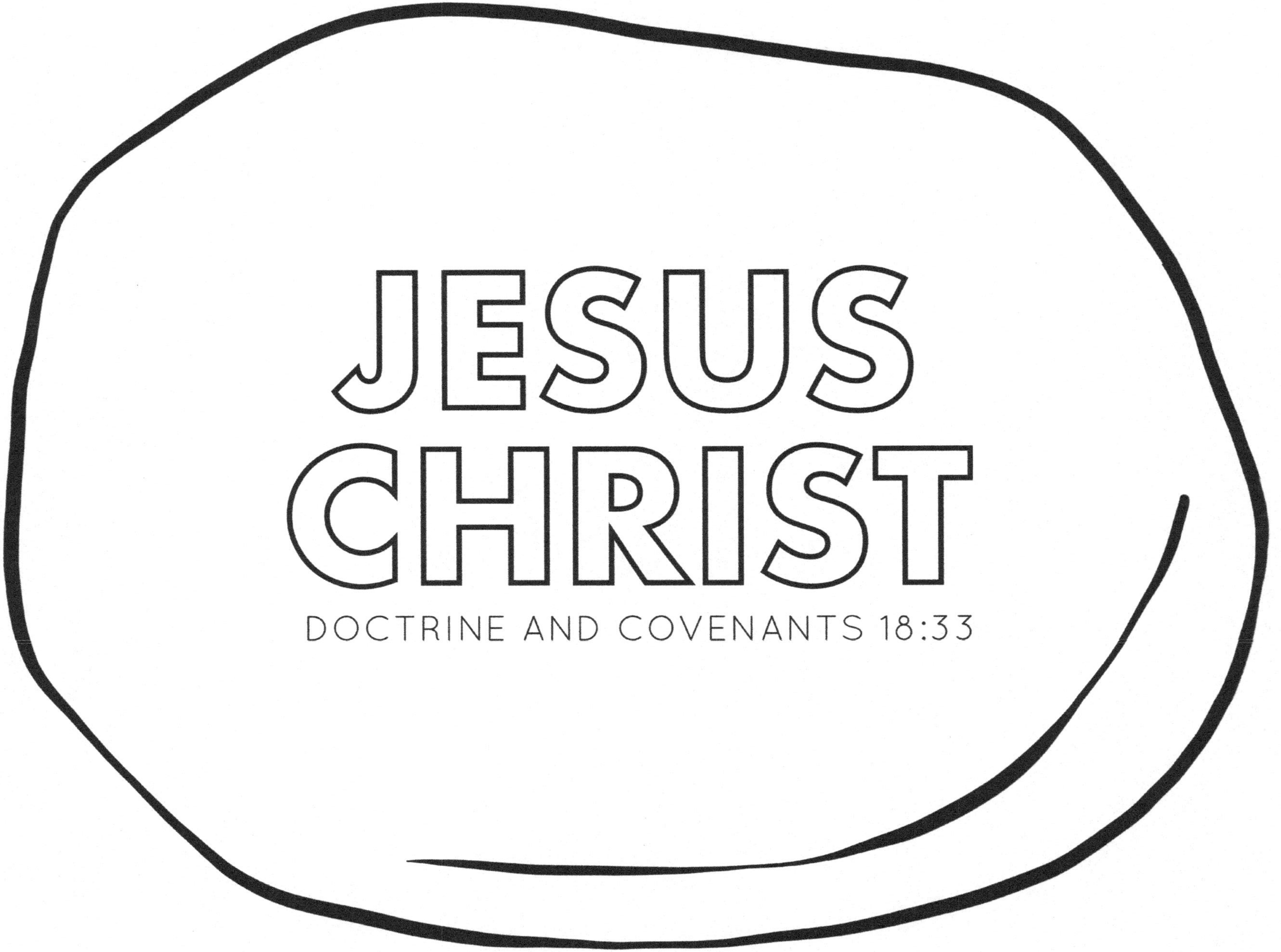

JEESUS CHRIST

DOCTRINE AND COVENANTS 18:33

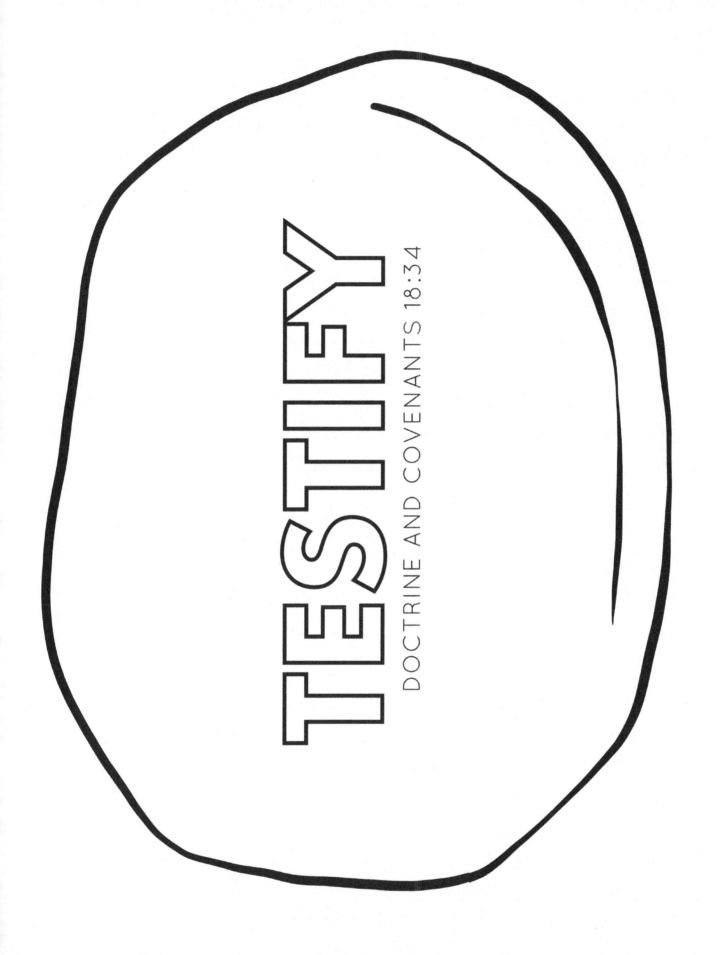

TESTIFY

DOCTRINE AND COVENANTS 18:34

SPIRIT

DOCTRINE AND COVENANTS 18:35

TESTIFY

DOCTRINE AND COVENANTS 18:36

GO & DO Family Activity

Sharing the Gospel of Jesus Christ Can Bring Joy
D&C 18:15-16; 44

In D&C 18:15-16; 44 we are told that sharing the Gospel of Jesus Christ can bring joy! We are also told that Heavenly Father will "work a marvelous work" by our hands (v.44). With your family watch this message from President Nelson where he invites the youth to experience the joy of missionary service.

A Prophetic Call: Experience the Joy of Missionary Service

Sometimes we don't know what impact we have until later on, but our Heavenly Father knows and loves it when we make an effort to follow His guidance.

As a family think of some ways you can joyfully share the gospel. After brainstorming, pick one idea and try it this week.

Here are some examples if you need some help getting started:

- Email family or friends or post a scripture on your social media.

- Text a family member or friend a quote from General Conference.

- Draw a nice picture for someone having a hard time.

- Invite a friend to sacrament meeting or primary.

- Be an example by smiling at people throughout the day.

- Do an act of service for a neighbor.

- Make a special treat for someone you want to get to know better.

- Forgive someone who was mean to you.

Follow the North Star

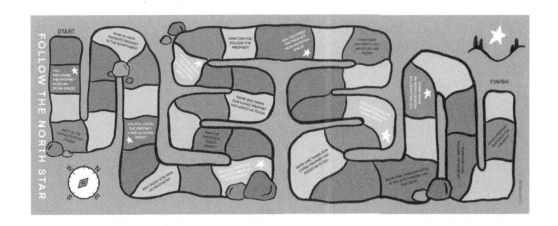

Instructions:

Cut out the hikers along the solid black lines and make a slit on the double lines at the bottom of the game pieces. Insert the rectangular pieces into the slits to make the characters stand up. Have each child choose a character.

To play the game, roll a die and move that many spaces. The stars on the board game represent obedience to the prophets.

If you land on a star or answer a question correctly, move ONE extra space.

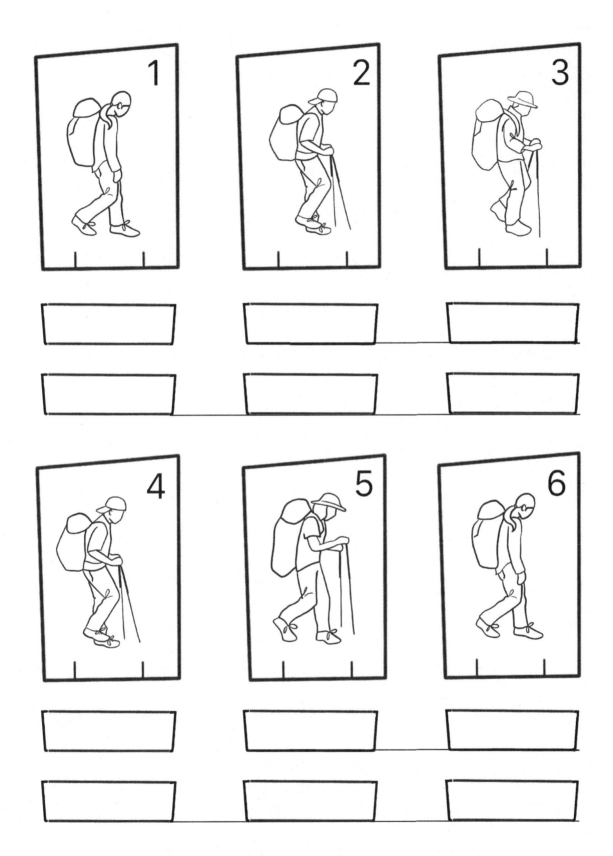

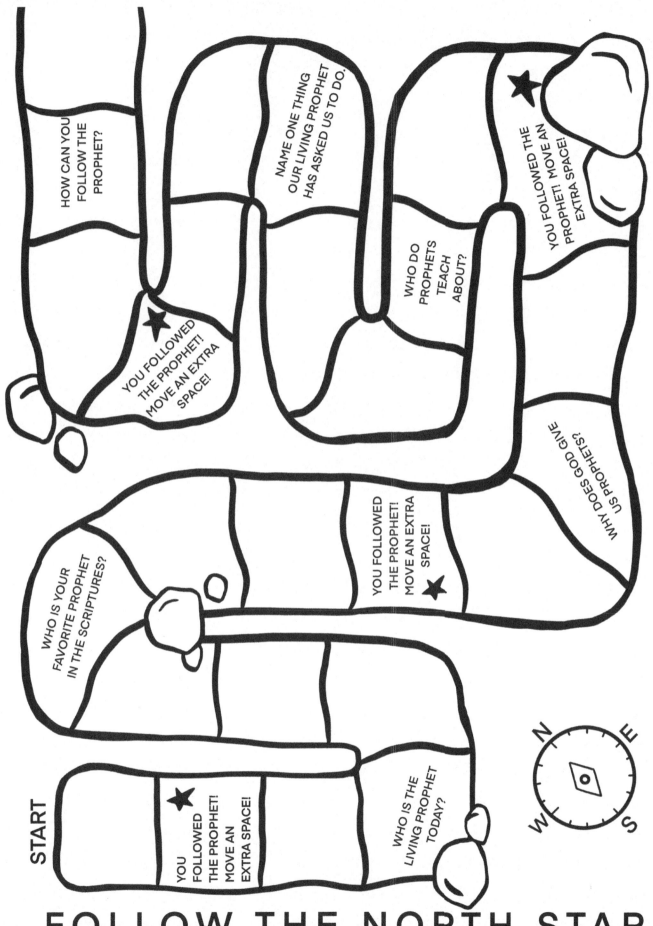

HOW CAN YOU FOLLOW THE PROPHET?

NAME ONE THING OUR LIVING PROPHET HAS ASKED US TO DO.

YOU FOLLOWED THE PROPHET! MOVE AN EXTRA SPACE!

WHO DO PROPHETS TEACH ABOUT?

YOU FOLLOWED THE PROPHET! MOVE AN EXTRA SPACE!

WHY DOES GOD GIVE US PROPHETS?

YOU FOLLOWED THE PROPHET! MOVE AN EXTRA SPACE!

WHO IS YOUR FAVORITE PROPHET IN THE SCRIPTURES?

START

YOU FOLLOWED THE PROPHET! MOVE AN EXTRA SPACE!

WHO IS THE LIVING PROPHET TODAY?

N E S W

FOLLOW THE NORTH STAR

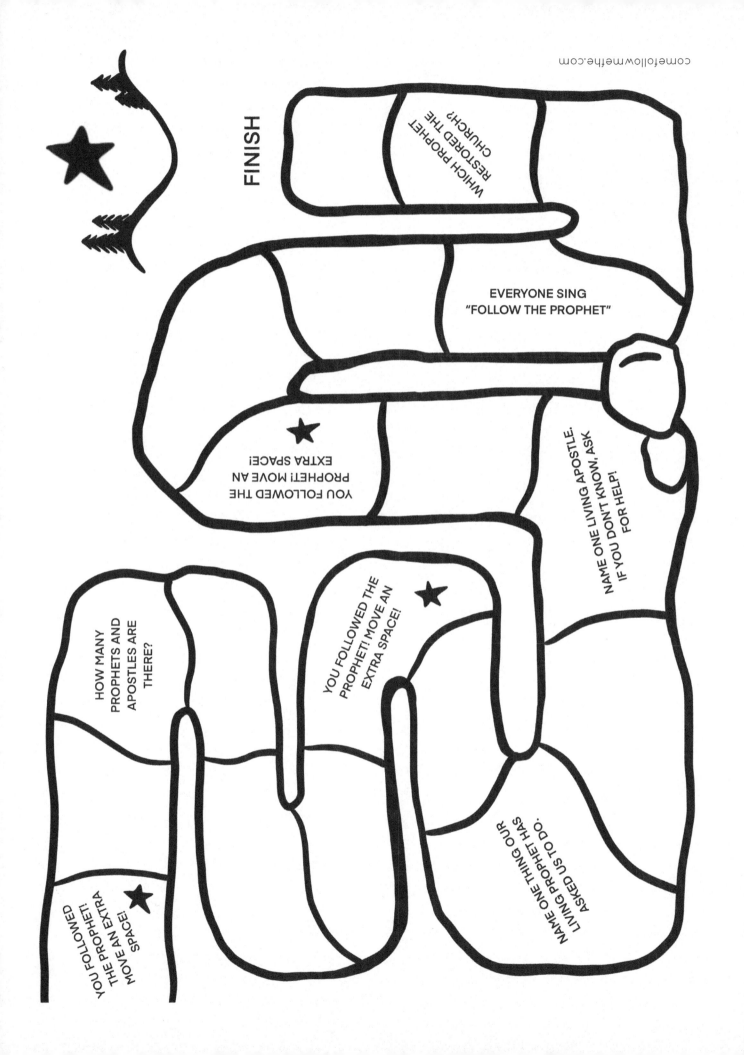

FINISH

WHICH PROPHET RESTORED THE CHURCH?

EVERYONE SING "FOLLOW THE PROPHET"

NAME ONE LIVING APOSTLE. IF YOU DON'T KNOW, ASK FOR HELP!

YOU FOLLOWED THE PROPHET! MOVE AN EXTRA SPACE!

HOW MANY PROPHETS AND APOSTLES ARE THERE?

YOU FOLLOWED THE PROPHET! MOVE AN EXTRA SPACE!

NAME ONE THING OUR LIVING PROPHET HAS ASKED US TO DO.

YOU FOLLOWED THE PROPHET! MOVE AN EXTRA SPACE!

Media Page

Videos and music are a highly effective way for children to learn Come, Follow Me. On this page, you'll find videos and songs that correlate with the lessons each week and can help aid in your family's understanding of the scriptures.

Use social media such as blogging, texting, and other forms of communication to share your testimony of the gospel to all the world.

Read about it here: D&C 18:15-16

Sharing Your Beliefs

This adaptation of the "Starfish Story" was originally written by Loren Eiseley in 1969. It reminds us that the worth of a soul is great in the eyes of our Heavenly Father, and that it's important to make a difference in people's lives even if our actions only impact just one person.

Read about it here: D&C 18:10

The Starfish Story

Elder Patrick Kearon was the newest member of the Quorum of the Twelve Apostles of The Church of Jesus Christ of Latter-day Saints on December 7, 2023. He was ordained later that day. Watch this video as he reflects on this calling as an Apostle of The Lord Jesus Christ.

Read about it here: D&C 18:27

Elder Patrick Kearon called to the Quorum of the Twelve Apostles

SONGS

My Heavenly Father Loves Me

Come With Me to Primary

We'll Bring the World His Truth

*If you are looking at this digitally, you can click the blue highlighted links and they will take you directly to the webpage. If you print this, you can open the camera on your phone, hover over the QR code and click the yellow box to open the video or song.

#1 Fan T-shirt Craft

Materials:
Old or new t-shirts (one per family member)
Markers (can use Sharpie or fabric markers)

For this activity, you are going to have everyone make their own "#1 Fan" T-shirt for someone else in your family. You can focus on one family member who is having a hard time or might have a challenge coming up in their life, or you can draw names so everyone in the family gets a #1 Fan shirt made about them.

Get your T-shirts out and write kind things about the person on them. You can draw some of their favorite things, use their favorite colors, draw hearts and smiley faces or write something kind about them. Make a #1 fan shirt for them so when you wear it and they see it, they know it's about them!

Examples to help get you started:
Mom is #1!
I love Rosie!
Aunt Joni Fan Club!
Best. Dad. Ever. (or Mom, kid,
son, daughter, etc.)

After making and trying on your T-shirts, read Doctrine and Covenants 18:10.
Explain that when we look at people with our eyes we see them how the world sees them (short/tall, glasses/no glasses, freckles, etc.). But when we look through God's eyes, everyone is of great worth! Heavenly Father loves all of His children. He is your #1 fan! It's good to celebrate each other and remind each other that we have worth even when we have a bad day, make a mistake or go through a hard time.

"The Worth of Souls is Great"

February 24-March 2
Doctrine & Covenants 18

Supplies

colored pencils, crayons or markers
baby pictures
timer

sticky notes
picture of Christ

I Am a Child of God

Gather baby pictures of each of your family members. Lay out the pictures and ask your child to identify who is in each picture. Talk about favorite memories that you have from when your child was born and express your love for them. Teach that we also have a Father in Heaven who loves us! We are His spirit children! He cares for us just like parents care for their children. Read D&C 18:10. Explain that everyone is a child of God! He loves each person! As you sing "I Am a Child of God" (Children's Songbook, p. 301) have your child hold up their picture. With your child, cut out and color the **"I Am a Child of God" frame**. Tape your child's picture to the frame and display it in your home.

Nursery Accommodation: Start by singing or listening to "I Am a Child of God." You could have the children stand up and dance to get wiggles out before they sit down for the lesson. Once the song is over, invite the children to sit down. Read D&C 18:10, and invite the children to make pretend glasses with their hands while you read the scripture. Teach that Heavenly Father loves us, and that we are His children. He sees the best in us. Invite each child, one by one, to come to the front and stand by you. Say the child's name and invite all to repeat "(Name) is a Child of God!" Do this for each child in the class. If you have a large class, you could split the group into two and assign a nursery leader to each. Once you've done this, have the children color a picture of themselves in the **"I Am a Child of God" frame**. It will just be scribbles and that's okay! Close by singing "I Am a Child of God" again.

I Can Take the Name of Christ Upon Me

Before the lesson, collect sticky notes and a picture of Christ. Start by reading D&C 18:21 and invite your child to clap when they hear the mystery word! The mystery word is "name." Explain that when we get baptized we take upon us the name of Christ. That means that we do all that we can to be like Him. Teach that even though we don't get baptized until we are 8 years old, we can still practice taking upon us the name of Christ by trying our best to be like Him. Set a timer for 3 minutes and together come up with words to describe Christ and write them down on the sticky notes. To help with wiggles, you could place the picture of Christ on the floor a small distance away and have your child run or walk to go stick the describing words on Christ. After doing this, have your child go and pick one of the attributes off of Christ and use that as something that you can work on doing to become like Christ. Then go and do something together that can help strengthen that characteristic. For example, if you use the word "kind" to describe Christ, go and do something kind like making a card for someone that is having a hard time. Close by singing "I'm Trying to be like Jesus" (Children's Songbook, p. 78).

"I am a Child of God" Frame

1. Cut out the frame and let your child color/decorate it.
2. Place a 4x6" photo of your child in the frame.
3. Display the framed picture in your home to remember that he/she is a child of God.

I am a child of God

I am a child of God

"Learn of Me"

March 3-9
Doctrine & Covenants 19

Supplies | crayons, colored pencils or markers | pen or pencil
pair of dice

 ### Scripture Study

Break the Code on prayer! Read D&C 19:38 and use the code to fill in the missing words in the scripture. Share your own personal experiences with praying always, and the feelings you have had after a prayer has been answered. (pg. 4)

 ### Go & Do Activity

Learn about the importance of repentance with a fun object lesson outside on a sunny day. Think about how the sun shining on our faces feels and how that is similar to the love of Heavenly Father. Read about the importance of keeping a relationship with Heavenly Father in D&C 19:16 and how the power of the Atonement helps us keep our sunny relationship. See our **Go & Do page** for details. (pg. 5)

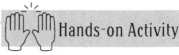 ### Hands-on Activity

Get your game dice ready for a fun family game night! Before you begin the game, make a list of people you know that may need some prayers at this time. Then play the **Roll & Pray game**. At the end of the game read D&C 19:38 and end with a family prayer, including the names of those individuals you wrote on your list. (pg. 6-8)

 ### Media Page

This week, you get to watch three videos:
1. Primary Kids Explain Prayer, 2. Principles of Peace: Repentance and
3. Hear Him: Listen to the Voice of Christ. Plus, you'll also learn these three songs: 1. Learn of Me,
2. Gethsemane and 3. Did You Think to Pray? See our **media page** to enjoy these as a family. (pg. 9)

 ### Surprise Activity

It's time to move and groove! **Simon Says** is a fun way to learn key words in D&C 19:23, and how our actions help us learn, listen and walk with Jesus Christ. Everlasting peace is our promise if we do these actions. Have fun and try to memorize the scripture while you play! (pg. 10)

 ### Coloring Page

Pull out your favorite markers and crayons and create a beautiful scripture poster! Highlight the action words and how you as a family can learn, listen and walk in the Spirit and with Jesus Christ as you color the **D&C 19:23 word art coloring page**. Everlasting peace comes to those who follow Christ. (pg. 11-12)

*We also have Church History Basket Books that are great for learning about significant events in the Doctrine and Covenants. They are especially helpful for young learners. Check them out in our shop!

*Remember, subscribers always get 40% off digital products in our shop and free shipping on any physical products!

BREAK THE CODE

ALWAYS, AND I WILL POUR OUT MY ___ ___ ___ ___ ___

___ ___ ___ ___ UPON YOU, AND ___ ___ ___ ___ SHALL BE YOUR BLESSING

- YEA, EVEN MORE THAN IF YOU SHOULD ___ ___ ___ ___ ___ ___ ___ ___ OF EARTH AND

___ ___ ___ ___ ___ ___ ___ ___ ___ CORRUPTIBLENESS TO THE EXTENT THEREOF.

D&C 19:38

www.comefollowmefhe.com

A - !
B - ?
C -
D - @
E - #
F -
G - %
H -
I - &
J - *
K - +
L -
M -]
N -
O - {
P -
R -
S - /
T -
U -
V - }
W -
X -
Y -
Z - ∞

Go & Do Family Activity

Repentance
D&C 19:16

Take your family outside and ask everyone to find a sunny spot. Stand or sit in the sun for a few moments. Ask your family "When did you feel the warmth of the sun?" They should have been able to feel it instantly. Ask them how it feels? If the weather is cold, you can also do this with a heater or a light/flashlight.

Now, cover or shade the sun using an umbrella/blanket so you are in full shade. Ask how they feel now? Ask "When did you stop feeling the warmth of the sun?" They should answer they felt a difference once the umbrella/blanket or barrier was placed between them and the sun.

Just like the sun, our Heavenly Father wants us to be in His direct path. If we put up barriers, like making mistakes or forgetting to keep the commandments, we have placed a barrier between us and Heavenly Father. Just like the umbrella/blanket with the sun.

When we are in the shade it is really hard to think about or imagine what it would be like to be in the sun. We are so focused on being in the shade and cold. To feel the sun again, we have to bring down the barriers, or repent, and open the connection with Heavenly Father again. As a family read D&C 19:16.

The only way we can remove the barrier is by repenting and removing it ourselves. No one else can remove the barrier for us. Because of Jesus Christ's Atonement, we are blessed with the commandments to repent and keep our close relationship with Heavenly Father. Once the barrier has been removed you will instantly feel the sun or the forgiveness will be instant.

Invite your family to share experiences of when they have pulled down a barrier and felt the warmth of Heavenly Father and Jesus Christ's Atonement.

We are all children of Heavenly Father and He wants us as His sons and daughters to be close to Him and His warm relationship, just like sitting in the sunshine and feeling the warmth of the sun's rays on our faces.

Roll & Pray Game

Needed for this game:

* A pair of dice
* 1 pen/writing utensil
* Each player needs their own Roll & Pray List sheet.

Rules:

* Sit in a circle or around a table.
* Place the pen in the middle of the circle.
* Take turns rolling the dice. Each person will roll 1 time, then pass the dice counterclockwise around the circle.
* Continue around the table until someone gets doubles.
* When you roll doubles, grab the pen (either from the table or from whoever has it) and start writing your list of things to pray for.
* The dice continue around the circle while a person writes.
* As soon as another set of doubles is rolled, that person grabs the pen from the person currently using it and begins writing.
* The first person to finish both lists, WINS!!

Roll & Pray
When you roll doubles- grab the pen and start making your prayer list!

Thanks for	Ask for
1.	1.
2.	2.
3.	3.
4.	4.
5.	5.
6.	6.
7.	7.
8.	8.
9.	9.
10.	10.

comefollowmefhe.com

Roll & Pray

When you roll doubles- grab the pen and
start making your prayer list!

Thanks for	Ask for
1.	1.
2.	2.
3.	3.
4.	4.
5.	5.
6.	6.
7.	7.
8.	8.
9.	9.
10.	10.

comefollowmefhe.com

Media Page

Videos and music are a highly effective way for children to learn Come, Follow Me. On this page, you'll find videos and songs that correlate with the lessons each week and can help aid in your family's understanding of the scriptures.

We are taught from a young age to pray to Heavenly Father, but do you know why? Enjoy this video of primary-aged children explaining why and when they pray. As a family, teach and discuss how you can pray more as a family and individually.
Read about it here: D&C 19:38

Primary Kids Explain Prayer

Everyone makes mistakes and will continue to make mistakes throughout life. Through the Atonement of Jesus Christ, we know we can repent and overcome our imperfections. Teach and discuss how Jesus Christ's sacrifice and death allow us as imperfect souls to return to his presence. Share examples of times in life you have used repentance and how it made you feel.
Read about it here: D&C 19:16-18

Principles of Peace: Repentance

The world is a loud and busy place. It is often difficult to slow down and feel the Spirit. When we turn our hearts to Jesus Christ, we can hear him and feel closer to him in our daily lives. After watching this video, discuss how as a family you can find time to power down and #hearhim. For older children, share the video and #hearhim with family and friends.
Read about it here: D&C 19:23

Hear Him: Listen to the Voice of Jesus Christ

SONGS

Learn of Me	Gethsemane	Did You Think to Pray?

*If you are looking at this digitally, you can click the blue highlighted links and they will take you directly to the webpage. If you print this, you can open the camera on your phone, hover over the QR code and click the yellow box to open the video or song.

SIMON SAYS

Get ready to play a fun game of Simon Says! In D&C 19:23, we read:

"Learn of me, and listen to my words; walk in the meekness of my Spirit, and you shall have peace in me."

We will play Simon Says with the action and result words from this scripture (learn, listen, walk). Let's practice them first.

LEARN: Place pointer finger to head.
LISTEN: Cup both hands and hold by both ears.
WALK: Move legs & arms to a walking position (think of the crosswalk sign).
PEACE: Bring both hands together in a prayer position, or the classic two-finger peace sign.

Begin by saying "Simon Says..." with one of the action words. Try to stump your family by going faster and faster with the words. After a few rounds, sit down with your family and discuss how learning, listening and walking are action words. We can learn of Christ, listen to Christ, walk with Christ, and forever have the spirit and peace if we do these things.

LEARN OF ME
LISTEN
TO MY WORDS
WALK
IN THE
MEEKNESS
OF MY SPIRIT
AND
HAVE PEACE
IN ME.

DOCTRINE &
COVENANTS 19:23

comefollowmefhe.com

"Learn of Me"

March 3-9
Doctrine & Covenants 19

Supplies

colored pencils, crayons or markers
scissors
clear casserole dish

picture of Christ
pepper
water

dish soap

I Can Repent

Before the lesson, collect the materials needed for the **repentance experiment**. Explain that today you are going to learn about repentance. Have your child say "repent." To repent means to make a change each day to become more and more like Jesus. Explain that sometimes we make wrong choices and when we make wrong choices it makes it hard to have the spirit with us and it's hard to feel good. Teach that Jesus loves us and made it so that if we repent, or choose to make things right and better, He will forgive us, help us feel good again and help us have the spirit with us again. Explain that repenting helps us become more like Jesus. Read D&C 19:16 and invite your child to clap when they hear the word "repent." As a family do the repentance experiment together. Discuss what is happening. Bear your testimony of the power of repentance.

Coloring Page

Don't forget to use the **coloring page** for this week as part of your lesson. It aligns with Doctrine & Covenants 19:23.

Music and videos are great for this age! Check out our media page for music and videos for this week.

I Can Learn of Jesus

Before the lesson, print out the pages for the **"I Can Learn of Jesus" mini book** and place them in different parts of your home, or outside for your Jesus walk. (As you are on your Jesus walk, you will collect the pages to be able to assemble the book.) Start by reading D&C 19:23 together. You can assign actions to the words: "learn of me" hold out your hands like a book; "listen to my words" cup your ear with your hands; "walk in the meekness" walk in place; "ye shall have peace" put prayer hands by your heart. Read this through a couple of times while doing the actions. Explain that Jesus tells us that we need to learn about Him, and He promises us that when we learn about Him, we will have peace. That means we will feel good and calm inside. Say "today we are going to go for a Jesus walk and learn more about Him." As a family, go for your Jesus walk and collect the pages for your book. Explain that another way you can learn about Jesus is by reading the scriptures. Share your testimony of Christ and His love for us. You could even share an experience you have had where Christ has brought you peace. Close by singing "Tell Me the Stories of Jesus" (Children's Songbook, pg. 57).

Nursery Accommodation: Before class print and assemble the **"I Can Learn of Jesus"** mini book. Read and do the actions for D&C 19:23 together. Have the children sit down and put their hands in their laps and explain that you are going to learn more about Jesus today. Read the Jesus story to them. Teach that when we think about Jesus and learn about Him, we have peace and feel happy. Watch and sing "Tell Me the Stories of Jesus" together.

Tell Me the Stories
of Jesus Sing-Along

Repentance Experiment
D&C 19:6

Materials:
Clear Casserole Dish or a dish with a clear bottom
Picture of Christ
Pepper
Water
Dish Soap

1. Put the picture of Christ underneath the dish. (To make it waterproof, you could stick it in a sheet protector sleeve).
2. Fill the dish with water.
3. Cover the surface of the water with pepper and explain how the pepper is like the wrong choices we make. Point out that when we make wrong choices it's hard to see and feel Christ or the Spirit.
4. Put some dish soap on your child's pointer finger. Teach that Christ gave us the special tool of repentance (like the soap).
5. Have your child touch the pepper with their soapy finger and watch how the pepper goes to the outside of the dish. Point out that when we choose to repent, Christ helps us make it better and then we can see Him and feel Him more through the spirit.

I CAN LEARN OF JESUS

1. JESUS IS MY SAVIOR AND HE CAN ALWAYS HELP ME.

2. JESUS PERFORMED MIRACLES LIKE HELPING THE BLIND TO SEE.

3. JESUS TAUGHT THE PEOPLE ABOUT LOVE AND KINDNESS TOO.

4. JESUS TOLD US TO FOLLOW HIM AND HE'D SHOW US WHAT TO DO.

5. JESUS LOVED THE CHILDREN AND SAT THEM ON HIS KNEE.

6. JESUS CALMED THE WATERS AND WALKED ACROSS THE SEA.

7. I CAN LEARN OF JESUS, AND HE PROMISES THAT IF I DO...

8. I WILL HAVE HIS PEACE WITH ME, I KNOW HIS PROMISES ARE TRUE.

"The Rise of the Church of Christ"

March 10-16
Doctrine & Covenants 20-22

Supplies | crayons, colored pencils or markers | random items to sort
picture of Christ for everyone | magazines | glue/tape

Scripture Study

As a family, read D&C 22 about baptizing with the correct authority. Then, have the person in your family who was most recently baptized share their experience. What happened? What feelings did they have? What was their favorite part? Who baptized them, and who gave them the authority to baptize? Finish by reading D&C 20:37 and share your testimony of baptism.

Go & Do Activity

Talk with your family about the Sacrament and how it is important to remember Jesus while we partake of the Sacrament. Have every member of your family pick a picture of Jesus Christ to look at during the Sacrament this coming Sunday. You can go to Deseret Book and have everyone choose a small size picture, or go online to the church website to print some. See our **Go & Do page** for details. (pg. 4)

Hands-on Activity

Gather random items from your house. For your lesson, have your children sort the items and this to how Joseph Smith received several revelations of how to organize the Church. Read D&C 20 and invite family members to share experiences passing the sacrament, taking the sacrament, preparing to be baptized or being baptized. See the **instruction page** for details. (pg. 5)

Media Page

This week, you get to watch three videos:
1. Sophia's Baptism Promises, 2. Chapter 9: Organization of the Church of Jesus Christ and 3. How The Church of Jesus Christ is Organized, Now You Know. Plus, you'll also learn these three songs: 1. The Church Of Jesus Christ, 2.When I Am Baptized and 3.The 4th Article of Faith. See our **media page** to enjoy these as a family. (pg. 6)

Surprise Activity

Read D&C 21:1-5. Use the **I Can Follow The Prophet collage page**, and let children rip pictures out of magazines, draw pictures, or use pictures of themselves to show ways that they are following the prophet. See the instruction page for details.(pg. 7)

Coloring Page

Read D&C 21:5 and talk about how our prophet speaks by the power of the Holy Ghost. Then let children color the **"For his word ye shall receive…" coloring page** while you talk about some things our prophet talked about in the last General Conference. (pg. 8-9)

*Hey! Do you want to have more meaningful gospel conversations? Teach your children basic gospel principles, like those found in the Articles of Faith, using our Bedtime Moments book.

*Remember, subscribers always get 40% off digital products in our shop and free shipping on any physical products!

GO & DO Family Activity

I can remember Jesus Christ while I partake of the Sacrament.
D&C 20:75-79

Every week we have the opportunity to hear the sacrament prayers. We get to witness to God that we are willing to take upon ourselves the name of Christ, always remember Him, and keep his commandments. In essence, every week we reaffirm and witness to God at the time of our baptism, we are renewing our baptismal covenant. With your family read D&C 20:75-79 and talk with your family about the sacrament and how important it is to remember Jesus Christ while we are partaking of the bread and water.

With your family watch this video by Elder L. Tom Perry about "Remembering the Sacrament."

Have every member of your family pick out a picture of Jesus Christ to look at during the sacrament this coming Sunday. You can go to Deseret Book and have everyone choose a small picture, or go online to the church website to print some out.

Revelation on Church Organization

For this hands-on activity, gather random items from around your house and put them in a bin. For example, balls, toy animals, silverware, clothes, etc. You will want to gather several items in each category so they can be organized/sorted.

Bring this bin to the lesson and dump it out. Explain that for these items to be most useful, they need to be organized. Say, "This is such a mess! Can we work together to organize this stuff?" Let your children sort the items.

After they have sorted all the items, relate this to how Joseph Smith received several revelations of how to organize the Church. He organized the Church in 1830. Read Doctrine and Covenants 20. Tell your family that because the Church is organized upon the Earth, we are blessed to be able to receive sacred ordinances, such as baptism, the sacrament and the sealing of families in the temple.

Invite family members to share experiences of passing the sacrament, taking the sacrament, preparing to be or being baptized. Then bear your testimony of the organization of the Church and how it is Christ's Church on the Earth today.

Media Page

Videos and music are a highly effective way for children to learn Come, Follow Me. On this page, you'll find videos and songs that correlate with the lessons each week and can help aid in your family's understanding of the scriptures.

Sophia learns how best to explain to her friend Ava the importance of the two-way promise she'll make with Heavenly Father during her baptism. These promises are called covenants.
Read about it here: D&C 20:37

Sophia's Baptism Promises

What happened on the day the church was organized? Joseph Smith received revelation on April 6, 1830, to organize the church. Watch this video to learn more about what happened that day.
Read about it here: D&C 21:3

Organization of the Church

God has used the same basic organizational structure for His Church throughout history. Jesus Christ is the head of The Church of Jesus Christ of Latter-day Saints. Prophets, apostles, and local leaders throughout the world work to serve Christ and assist all members as they develop stronger relationships with Him.
Read about it here: D&C 20:38-67

How the Church of Jesus Christ is Organized

SONGS

The Church of Jesus Christ

When I Am Baptized

The Fourth Article of Faith

*If you are looking at this digitally, you can click the blue highlighted links and they will take you directly to the webpage. If you print this, you can open the camera on your phone, hover over the QR code and click the yellow box to open the video or song.

MY FOLLOW THE PROPHET COLLAGE

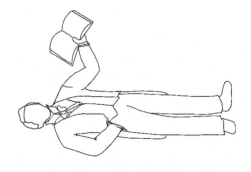

"For his word ye shall receive, as if from mine own mouth, in all patience and faith." -D&C 21:5

"The Rise of the Church of Christ"

March 10-16
Doctrine & Covenants 20-22

Supplies

colored pencils, crayons or markers
clear page protectors, lamination
or plastic wrap

playdough
scissors
hole punch

shoelace or yarn+tape

I Am on Christ's Team

Show your child a team jersey or uniform. Let your child try it on! (If you don't have a jersey, show a picture of someone wearing a jersey.) Explain that when someone wears this jersey, it shows that they are a member of a team! They represent the team and work together with other team members to do their best. Show a picture of Jesus Christ. Teach that we become members of Jesus Christ's team when we join His true church. We do not wear a jersey, instead, we get baptized, follow Christ's example and teach others about His gospel. Place the **playdough mats** into clear page protectors, laminate or cover with plastic wrap. With your child, recreate the images by pressing playdough onto the mats. Share what blessings you receive from being on Christ's team.

I Can Remember Jesus During the Sacrament

Before reading, invite your child to touch their nose if they have heard these scriptures before. Read D&C 20:77 and D&C 20:79. Teach that the sacrament is a special time when we think about Jesus. Jesus did many wonderful things for us. Jesus made it so that we can repent, and so that we can live with Heavenly Father and our families forever! When we get baptized, we make a special promise with Jesus called a covenant. That means we make promises to Jesus and He makes promises to us. Explain that even though your child isn't baptized yet, they can still think about those promises. Teach your child how to remember Jesus with the **Sacrament Lacing Cards**. (See instruction page for details.)
Keep the lacing cards in your church bag and allow your child to look at them during the sacrament so that they can remember the promises they make. You can also review the motions as another tool to remember. You could even play charades with the motions!
Nursery Accommodation: Follow the plan for the Sacrament Lacing Cards. For each hand motion, have the children stand up to do it.

Coloring Page

Don't forget to use the **coloring page** for this week as part of your lesson. It aligns with Doctrine & Covenants 21:5.

Additional Resources

Don't forget that videos are great for this age! Be sure to check out the **media page** for music and videos for this week.

*Remember, subscribers always get 40% off all digitial products in the shop!

I Belong to the Church of Jesus Christ
PLAYDOUGH MATS

1. Place playdough mats inside clear page protectors, laminate or cover tightly with plastic wrap.
2. With your child, make shapes with the playdough, pressing the playdough onto the mats. Decorate the crown, build a church house and form rectangles for the scriptures.

HOMEMADE PLAYDOUGH
1 cup flour
1/4 cup salt
3/4 cup water
3 tbsp lemon juice
1 tbsp vegetable oil
Optional: food coloring or liquid scents

Directions:

In a medium, non-stick saucepan, heat the water, oil and lemon juice over medium heat until hot, but not boiling. Reduce heat to low.

In a bowl, combine the dry ingredients. Pour the dry ingredients into the hot water mixture, mixing to combine. Cook on low heat, stirring until it forms a ball and doesn't stick to the sides. Do not overcook.

Remove the pot from the heat and dump the playdough out onto wax paper to cool.

Knead for a few minutes once the playdough is cool enough to work with. Let the playdough cool completely before using.

I Belong to the Church of Jesus Christ

The Church of JESUS CHRIST of Latter-Day Saints

comefollowmefhe.com

Through faith and righteousness, I can receive a Crown of Eternal Life.

D&C 20:14

The Holy Scriptures are True

D&C 20:11

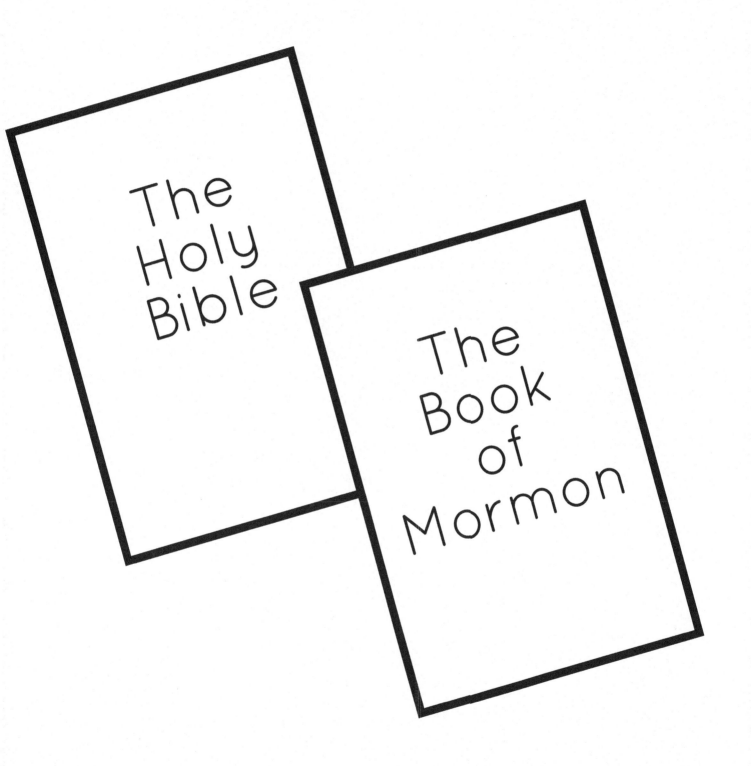

Sacrament Lacing Cards
D&C 20:77, 79

To prepare your lacing cards, print them on cardstock. Use a hole punch to cut out the holes. Cut a long strand of yarn or get some shoe laces. If you use yarn, wrap some tape around the ends to prevent them from fraying and make it easier for your child to thread the yarn through the holes.

Teach your children how each card can help them remember Jesus.
1. Show the first lacing card (always remember, child with a thought bubble of Christ). Explain that we promise to always remember Him. That means that we think of Jesus and try to be like Him. Put your pointer finger to your head and have your child repeat, "Always remember Him."
2. Show the second card (take His name upon us, missionary tag). Teach that we promise to take His name upon us. That means that we get baptized and then do all we can to be like Jesus. Put your hand over your heart and have your child repeat, "Take His name upon us."
3. Show the third lacing card (keep the commandments, commandment tablets). Explain that we promise to keep the commandments. That means that we follow Jesus and Heavenly Father and do what they teach us to do. We can learn about the commandments in the scriptures. Hold out one hand, put the other hand in a fist (like rock, paper, scissors). Pound three times on your hand and say, "Keep the commandments."
4. Show the fourth lacing card (spirit, quilt) and explain that when we keep our promises, Jesus promises that we will have the Spirit with us always! That is such a special thing because the spirit helps us so much. It helps us when we are sad, it keeps us safe and gives us calm and peaceful feelings. The Spirit can be like a warm blanket. Hug yourself and have your child repeat, "We will have the Spirit."

We recommend keeping the lacing cards in your church bag and allowing your child to look at them during the sacrament so that they can remember the promises they make.

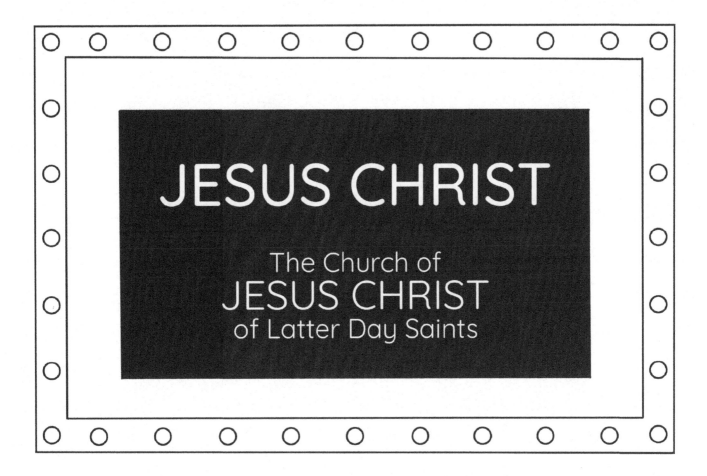

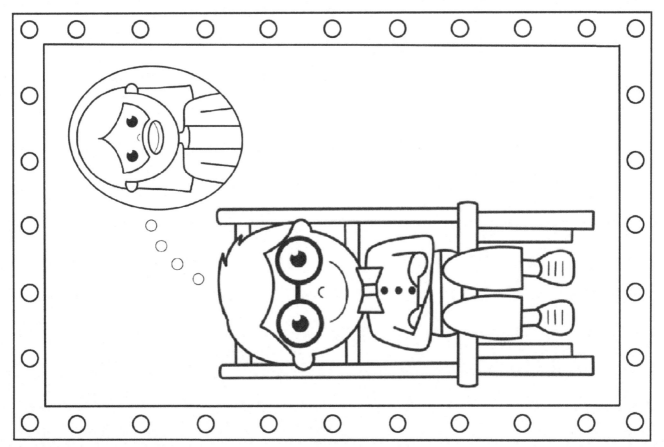

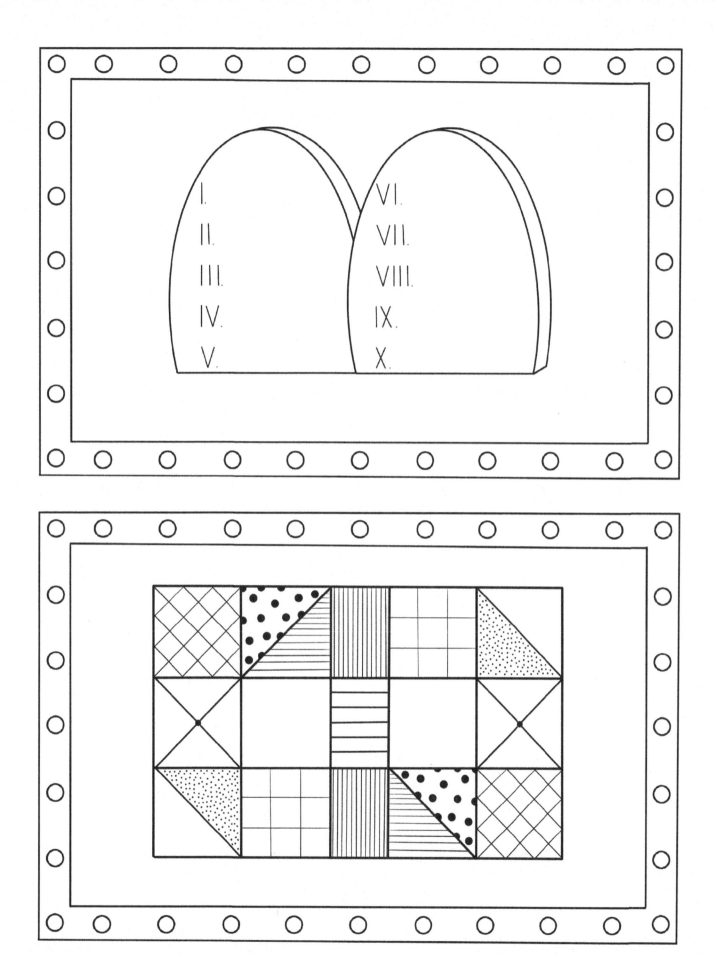

"Seek for the Things of a Better World"

March 17-23
Doctrine & Covenants 23-26

Supplies

crayons, colored pencils or markers
paper

scissors
glue/tape

Scripture Study

Dissect D&C 23 and draw, paint or write down what Heavenly Father asked the men in the scriptures to do. Think of their tasks and see if you are also called to do the same things as you live your life as a disciple of Jesus Christ.
You can also **Break the Code** for D&C 23:7.
(pg. 4)

Go & Do Activity

Although we may go through trials and tribulations, we can feel comfort in knowing the Lord is with us. Read about the Lord's comfort in D&C 24:8. Then go on a family outing to spread sunshine in the service of others to overcome your trials. See our **Go & Do page** for details. (pg. 5)

Hands-on Activity

Emma Smith was declared "an elect lady" in a revelation in D&C 25. Using the list of attributes in this chapter, compile and complete the "**An Elect Child" worksheet** with your family. Have each person pick one of the attributes to focus and work on this week. (pg. 6)

Media Page

This week, you get to watch three videos:
1. An Elect Lady, 2. If Thou Endure it Well and 3. Songs Sung and Unsung. Plus, you'll also learn these three songs: 1. Count Your Blessings, 2. Hum Your Favorite Hymn and
3. Pioneer Children Sang as They Walked. See our **media page** to enjoy these as a family. (pg. 7)

Surprise Activity

Think of times you have felt the Spirit through music. Music is a powerful tool in feeling the Spirit and converting us to the gospel of Jesus Christ, as taught in D&C 25. Get your lips ready for a fun, family-friendly **Hum Your Favorite Hymn game** focusing on the importance of how uplifting music draws us closer to Christ, and is a song of righteousness and a prayer. (pg. 8-13)

Coloring Page

Emma Smith was tasked with compiling the first hymnal for the church. In D&C 25 we read that the Lord delights in music!
Find your favorite hymns and sing them as a family while you color the "**...for my soul delighteth in the song of the heart..." coloring page** on uplifting and worthy music. (pg. 14-17)

*Do you have access to our Church History Read Alongs for Kids? They are a great way to help your children better understand what is happening in the Doctrine and Covenants!

*Remember, subscribers always get 40% off digital products in our shop and free shipping on any physical products!

comefollowmefhe.com

BREAK THE CODE

AND, BEHOLD, IT IS YOUR _____ TO _____

WITH THE TRUE CHURCH, AND GIVE YOUR LANGUAGE TO

_____ CONTINUALLY,

THAT YOU MAY RECEIVE THE _____

OF THE _____. AMEN.

D&C 23:7

www.comefollowmethe.com

A -
B -
C -
D -
E -
F -
G -
H -
H -
J -

K -
L -
M -
N -
O -
P -

Q -
R -
S -
T -
U -
V -
W -
X -
Y -
Z -

Go & Do Family Activity

The Savior can lift me up out of my afflictions.
D&C 24:8

In D&C 24:8 we read that we must be patient in our trials and afflictions. Think of a time you or your family had a struggle. Was it easy to be patient? Did you feel alone? The Lord promises that He is with us, no matter what. What can we do while we go through these trials? Richard G. Scott taught,

"I testify that when the Lord closes one important door in your life, He shows His continuing love and compassion by opening many other compensating doors through your exercise of faith. He will place in your path packets of spiritual sunlight to brighten your way. They often come after the trial has been the greatest, as evidence of the compassion and love of an all-knowing Heavenly Father. They point the way to greater happiness and more understanding and strengthen your determination to accept and be obedient to His will."

Think of the trial again. Did you see any of the "spiritual sunlight?"

Think of a family in your ward or community you could serve and provide "spiritual sunlight" for. Is there a family with young children you can sit with during sacrament meeting to help assist with? You can print coloring pages and pass them out to your friends and neighbors to help them with their FHE lessons. You can visit a few lonely people who would enjoy some sunshine. Cut out hearts or suns from construction paper and tape them on someone's door to "spread sunshine!"

Enjoy spreading sunshine and see how it makes you feel! Does serving others help you feel better in your trials and afflictions?

An Elect Child of God

Attribute

Definition

Where can I practice this attribute?

How can I practice this attribute?

Self Portrait

Attribute Challenge:

DAY 1	DAY 2	DAY 3	DAY 4	DAY 5	DAY 6	DAY 7

Media Page

Videos and music are a highly effective way for children to learn Come, Follow Me. On this page, you'll find videos and songs that correlate with the lessons each week and can help aid in your family's understanding of the scriptures.

Emma Smith was a remarkable woman. She was not only wife to the Prophet Joseph Smith, she was also the first Relief Society President. She had many trials and tribulations in her life, but was described in a revelation as "an elect lady". Learn more about Emma and her attributes as a family.
Read about it here: D&C 25

An Elect Lady

Robert D. Hales explains how he continued to have faith in Jesus Christ during his health trials. Although he felt sad and discouraged at times, he leaned on his faith and testimony to bear his burdens and ease the weight of his trial. It may be hard at the moment, but we can do all things through Jesus Christ who strengthens us.
Read about it here: D&C 24:8

If Thou Endure it Well

Enjoy a cartoon on Jeffrey R. Holland's talk on how we can remember, "...the Savior hears the songs you cannot sing." It takes many voices to build a choir and beautiful music. We need to be ourselves and join in the choir of the world to sing and show your worth daily. Don't forget that "...the loss of one voice diminishes every other singer in the mortal choir..."
Read about it here: D&C 23; 25

Songs Sung and Unsung

SONGS

Count Your Blessings

Hum Your Favorite Hymn

Pioneer Children Sang as They Walked

*If you are looking at this digitally, you can click the blue highlighted links and they will take you directly to the webpage. If you print this, you can open the camera on your phone, hover over the QR code and click the yellow box to open the video or song.

Hum Your Favorite Hymn

In Doctrine and Covenants 25, we learn that Emma Smith was an "elect lady" who was called by God "to write, to expound scriptures" and to "make a selection of sacred hymns." (D&C 25:11)

1. Print the hymn cards double-sided with the hymn book image page on the back. Cut out the cards and place them face down in a pile.

2. To play: draw a card (don't show anyone), hum the tune of the first line of the hymn listed on the card and see if anyone can guess which hymn it is.

3. If no one can guess after the first line is hummed, hum the next line and on until someone can guess the correct hymn.

*If you don't know the tune, you can pull it up in the Gospel Library app and play it.

Keep the Commandments p. 303	Love One Another p. 308	Love at Home p. 294
Nearer, My God, to Thee p. 100	Sweet Hour of Prayer p. 142	The Iron Rod p. 274
The Spirit of God p. 2	Lead, Kindly Light p. 97	Called to Serve p. 249

Come, Follow Me

p. 116

Families Can Be Together Forever

p. 300

God Be with You Till We Meet Again

p. 152

How Firm a Foundation

p. 85

How Great Thou Art

p. 86

I Know That My Redeemer Lives

p. 136

I Need Thee Every Hour

p. 98

Count Your Blessings

p. 241

I Stand All Amazed

p. 193

I Believe in Christ	Teach Me to Walk in the Light	I Am a Child of God
p. 134	p. 304	p. 301
Because I Have Been Given Much	Choose the Right	We Thank Thee, O God, for a Prophet
p. 219	p. 239	p. 19
Abide with Me	Be Still, My Soul	Come, Come, Ye Saints
p. 166	p. 124	p. 30

"...for my soul delighteth in the song of the heart..."

-D&C 25:12

HYMNS

comefollowmefhe.com

"Seek for the Things of a Better World"

March 17-23
Doctrine & Covenants 23-26

Supplies

colored pencils, crayons or markers
scissors
brad

slips of paper or sticky notes
optional: plastic eggs, rice, tape

I Like to Sing

Music Movement: Explain that music is an important part of the gospel of Jesus Christ. Music can bring us joy and help us learn! Emma Smith was asked to compile songs to be used in the church. In D&C 25:11, Emma is taught that Jesus Christ loves music! He teaches that His "soul delighteth in the song of the heart!" We can have the same feeling when we listen to or sing righteous music. For a fun and interactive game, learn "Sing a Song" (Children's Songbook, p. 253a). Use the **I Like to Sing spinner game**, changing the words, and adding movements to act out the different animals on the spinner. Have fun singing and moving together!

Coloring Page

Don't forget to use the **coloring page** for this week as part of your lesson. It aligns with Doctrine & Covenants 25.

Additional Resources

Our **Church History Basket Book** "Printing of the Book of Mormon" goes along great with this week's lesson. These books are a great resource, especially for young children!

Don't forget that videos are great for this age! Be sure to check out the **media page** for music and videos for this week.

*Remember, subscribers always get 40% off all digital products in the shop!

My Soul Delighteth Freeze Dance

Before the lesson, compile a list of your family's favorite Primary songs/hymns. Write them on strips of paper or sticky notes. As a family, read D&C 25:12-13. Teach that Heavenly Father and Jesus want us to be happy, and want us to have the spirit. Explain that good songs, like the ones we sing at church, help us have those good feelings. They make us feel delighted and rejoice, just like the scriptures teach us. Next, take the papers and sprinkle them on the floor. Play freeze dance to a fun wiggle song. Explain to your child that when they hear the music stop, they need to go and jump on one paper and that will be the song that you sing together as a family. You could even mix it up and sing some songs then watch the lyric videos for others. There are a lot of great videos with pictures on YouTube. You could also put together the **egg shakers** and shake them while you sing some of the songs. Play this game for as long as your child finds it enjoyable.

Nursery Accommodation: Write down songs on slips of paper. Make sure there's a good mix of reverent and wiggle songs. Instead of sprinkling the papers on the floor, you could hide them in the nursery room, or tape them to the board or wall, and invite one child at a time to pick a paper. During this time, you could even bring in egg shakers for the children to shake while you sing. These are great for the children's development as well as a good attention keeper! Make sure to read D&C 25:12-13 before beginning the activity. Have the children show you their happiest faces when you read the word "delighteth!"

I Like to Sing
Action Game

1. Construct the spinner by attaching the arrow to the game board with a brad.
2. Practice singing "Sing a Song" (Children's Songbook, pg. 253a). Change the words to play the action game, performing the actions while singing the song.
(A music-only version of the song can be downloaded from churchofjesuschrist.org)

Sing, Sing, Sing.
I like to sing!
I like to sing like a bird.
Sing, Sing, Sing! (Sing and wave arms to act like a bird.)

Run, run, run.
I like to run!
I like to run like a horse.
Run, Run, Run! (Run in a circle.)

Hop, Hop, Hop.
I like to hop.
 like to hop like a frog.
Hop, Hop, Hop! (Hop up and down.)

Stomp, Stomp, Stomp.
I like to stomp.
I like to stomp like an elephant.
Stomp, Stomp, Stomp! (Stomp your feet.)

Clap, Clap, Clap.
I like to clap.
I like to clap like a seal.
Clap, Clap. Clap.
(Clap your hands.)

RUN

HOP

SING

STOMP

CLAP

comefollowmethe.com

Easy Egg Shakers

Supplies Needed:
plastic eggs (one for each child)
rice, or other noise-making filler (beads, dry beans, etc.)
duct tape
scissors

To Make:
1. Fill one-half of the plastic egg with your noise-making filler.
2. Close and tape around the opening crease with your duct tape.
3. Make sure they are tightly sealed and have fun shaking them!!

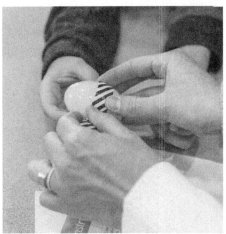

"All Things Must Be Done in Order"

March 24-30
Doctrine & Covenants 27-28

Supplies	crayons, colored pencils or markers paper	suit coat and tie scissors stapler	PB&J ingredients glue/tape

Scripture Study

Read D&C 27: 15-18 as a family. Then draw your own "sword of the spirit" and "shield of faith" by using the **drawing guides** to draw and design your own. You may want to draw the sword and shield for younger children and then let them color the picture. (pg. 4-5)

Go & Do Activity

Choose one family member to be the "prophet" that everyone will follow. Dress them up to look like our current prophet. Then play "Simon Says" as a family, but instead say, "The Prophet Says..." Play as many times as you want. After you finish, read D&C 28:2 and talk about a time when you were blessed by following the prophet. See our **Go & Do page** for details. (pg. 6)

Hands-on Activity

Read D&C 27:1-2. Discuss the importance of the sacrament. Explain that we need to focus on the Savior during the sacrament. Make **"My Sacrament Book."** Cut out the pages, then staple them in order. Children can use this to help them remember the Savior during the sacrament. (pg. 7-10)

Media Page

This week, you get to watch three videos: 1. Why Do We Have Prophets?, 2. Recognizing Revelation and 3. Sacrament. Plus, you'll also learn these three songs: 1. Tell Me, Dear Lord, 2. Latter-day Prophets and 3. The Holy Ghost. See our **media page** to enjoy these as a family. (pg. 11)

Surprise Activity

Have fun with this object lesson teaching your children how there is an order to things in Christ's church. See if your children can instruct you in making a peanut butter and jelly sandwich. Then complete the **All Things Must be Done in Order cut and paste activity**. See the instruction page for details. (pg. 12-16)

Coloring Page

Explain how the members of the church used to drink wine, not water, for the sacrament. One day, when Joseph Smith went to buy wine for Sunday, he received a revelation that he shouldn't buy wine or strong drink. Read D&C 27:2 and discuss how it's important that we remember Jesus Christ during the sacrament as you color the **sacrament tray coloring page** together. (pg. 17-18)

*Hey! Do you want to have more meaningul gospel conversations? Teach your children basic gospel principles, like those found in the Articles of Faith, using our Bedtime Moments book.

*Remember, subscribers always get 40% off digital products in our shop and free shipping on any physical products!

The Shield of Faith

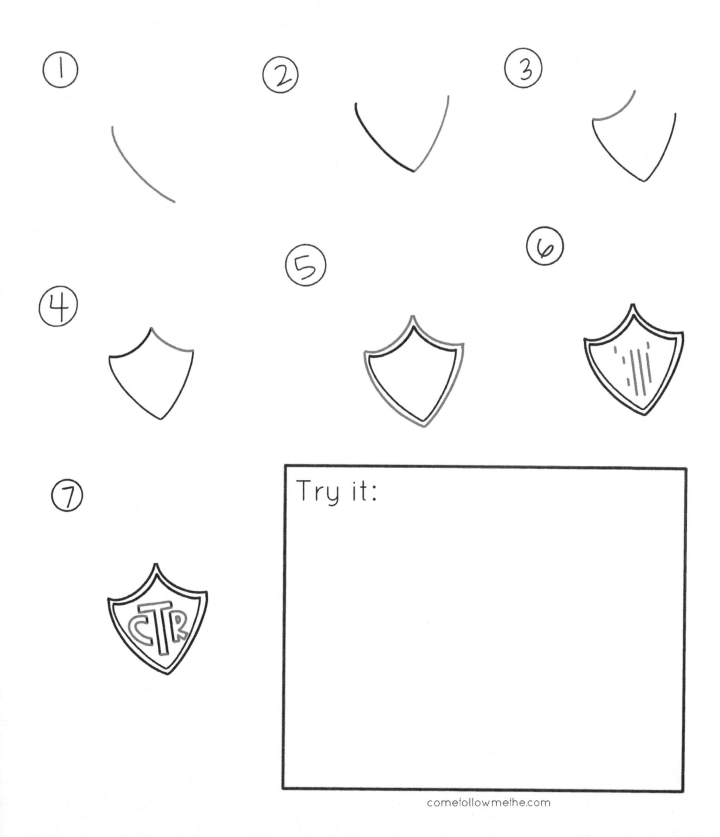

Try it:

HOW TO DRAW
The Sword of the Spirit

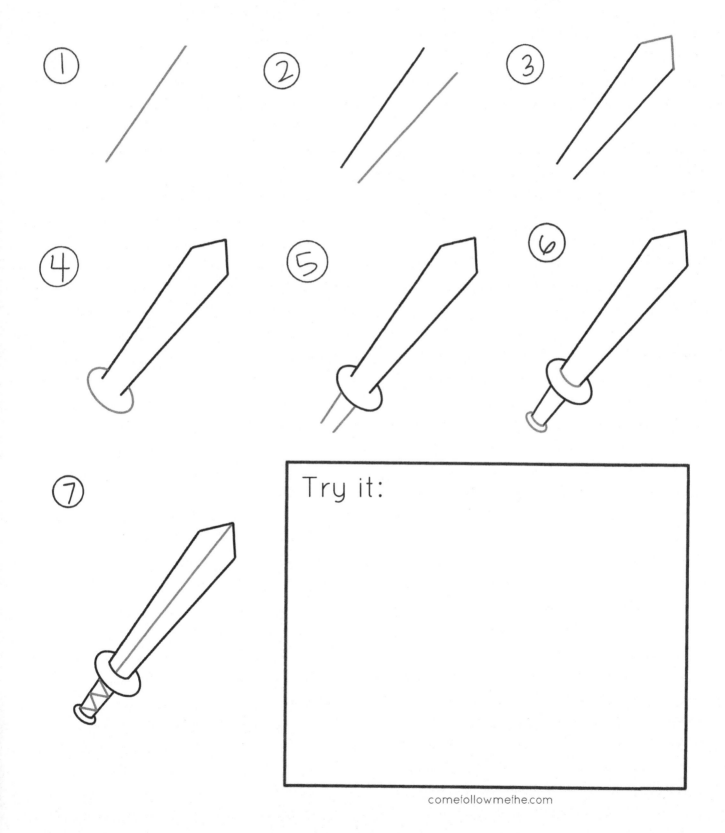

Try it:

comefollowmethe.com

Go & Do Family Activity

The prophet leads the church.
D&C 28:2

What would it be like if anyone could receive commandments and revelation for the entire church? Imagine the confusion there would be in the church. When Hiram Page claimed to have received a revelation for the church it caused great confusion among the early saints. In D&C 28 Heavenly Father revealed an order for revelation in His church.

Choose one family member to be the "prophet" that everyone will follow. Dress them up to look like our current prophet. Get an old suit coat and tie to have them wear. If you really want to commit, you can make them look older by using makeup to draw on wrinkles, gray hair color spray or even a bald cap!

To start, have your leader "prophet" stand in front of everyone and say, "The prophet says, "(give an action like pat your head)" like in the game 'Simon Says'. Everyone follows until the leader "prophet" doesn't say, "The prophet says" when they give direction. Then everyone playing freezes and doesn't do the action. If someone does follow the action you can say, " The prophet didn't say!"

Finish up the activity by reading D&C 28:2 and talk about a time when you were blessed after following the direction from the prophet. You could also go to the most recent General Conference and review what the prophet has taught us to do. Make a plan as a family to follow this direction.

Supplies Needed:

* Prophet Dress up (ex. tie, old suit coat)

My Sacrament Book

I can remember Jesus during the sacrament.

D&C 21:1-2

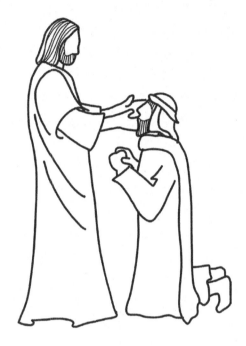

He heals.

He loves all.

He was a child who learned the scriptures.

He was baptized
as an example to us.

He gave us
commandments.

He redeemed us all.

He taught with love.

Media Page

Videos and music are a highly effective way for children to learn Come, Follow Me. On this page, you'll find videos and songs that correlate with the lessons each week and can help aid in your family's understanding of the scriptures.

God used prophets in biblical times to relay His message and teach His children. Today, that same God is still calling prophets.
Read about it here: D&C 2:7

Why Do We Have Prophets?

Sometimes when we pray, it can be hard to know what Heavenly Father is trying to tell us. Ashlee must learn the difference between her own feelings and the peace that comes from the Holy Ghost. Jesus Christ promises us peace to guide us through life.
Read about it here: D&C 28:2

Recognizing Revelation

We asked kids to tell us the story of the Last Supper in their own words and to explain why it matters for our lives today.
Read about it here: D&C 27:2

Sacrament

SONGS

Tell Me, Dear Lord

Latter Day Prophets

The Holy Ghost

*If you are looking at this digitally, you can click the blue highlighted links and they will take you directly to the webpage. If you print this, you can open the camera on your phone, hover over the QR code and click the yellow box to open the video or song.

All Things Must be Done in Order

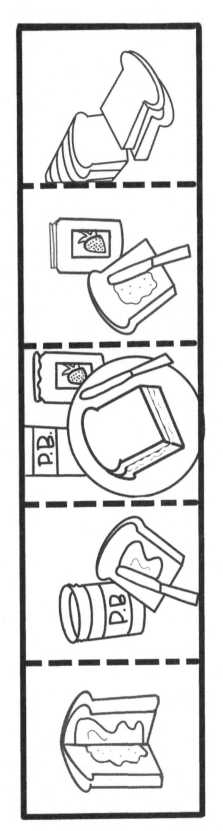

Cut out each square and glue them in the right order on the other page.

All Things Must be Done in Order

1	2	3	4	5

Just like there is a certain order when you make a peanut butter and jelly sandwich, God has an order in how He reveals new revelation for His church.

1	2	3	4	5

Revelation for the Church of Jesus Christ of Latter-day Saints comes to our living prophet..

comefollowmefhe.com

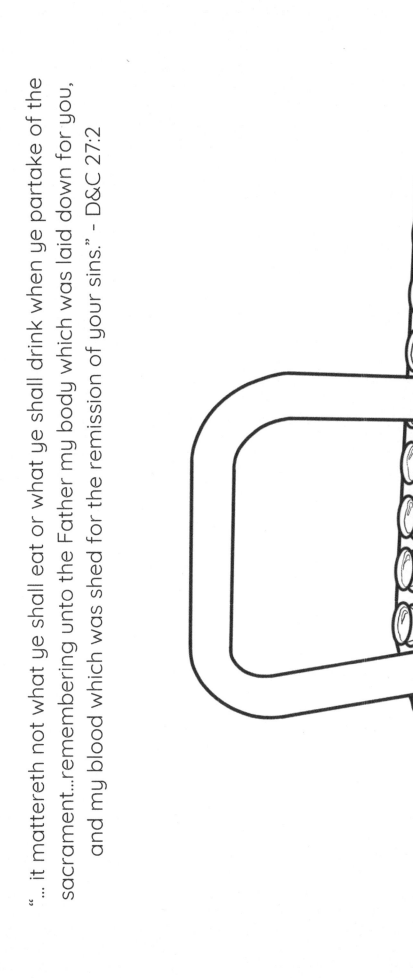

" ... it mattereth not what ye shall eat or what ye shall drink when ye partake of the sacrament...remembering unto the Father my body which was laid down for you, and my blood which was shed for the remission of your sins." – D&C 27:2

"All Things Must Be Done in Order"

March 24-30
Doctrine & Covenants 27-28

Supplies

colored pencils, crayons or markers
scissors
glue/tape

die
paper strips
stapler with staples

I Can Put on the Armor of God

Heavenly Father loves us so much. Because He loves us, He wants us to be safe and make good choices. In the scriptures, we learn to put on the whole armor of God. Read D&C 27:15. Armor keeps us safe. When we put on the armor of God, we do things that will help us make good choices. Making good choices keeps our spirit safe, and when our spirit is safe, we can have the Holy Ghost with us. The scriptures teach us that when we put on the armor of God, we can be happy! Play the **Put on the Armor of God game** together. When finished, bear testimony of the power of putting on the whole armor of God.

Coloring Page

Don't forget to use the **coloring page** for this week as part of your lesson. It aligns with Doctrine & Covenants 27:2.

Additional Resources

Don't forget that videos are great for this age! Be sure to check out the **media page** for music and videos for this week.

*Remember, subscribers always get 40% off all digital products in the shop!

I Can Follow the Prophet

Start by singing "Follow the Prophet" (Children's Songbook, pg. 110). You can march around to make it fun! Invite your child to sit and show them a picture of the prophet. Ask them if they know who it is. Explain that this is the prophet! Heavenly Father calls a prophet. The prophet is Heavenly Father and Jesus' special helper that leads our church. Heavenly Father gives the prophet special tools to help Him lead the church. Read D&C 28:7. Explain that when we follow the prophet, we will be happy! Share some of the teachings from the prophet with your child. Explain that general conference is coming soon! General conference is a special time when we get to hear the prophet! Make a paper chain countdown to the conference together, and remove a link from it each day as you get closer to the conference. Share your testimony of the prophet and the blessings that come from following the prophet.

Nursery Accommodation: Follow the outline for the lesson above. If you want, you could make a paper chain for each child before class and let them color on it after the lesson. If you want to forgo the paper chain, after bearing testimony of the prophet, sing "Follow the Prophet" again. Mix up the actions to this song. For example, instead of marching around the room, you could have the children jump up and say, "Follow the Prophet!" when they hear it in the song.

PUT ON THE ARMOR OF GOD GAME

PRACTICE PUTTING ON THE WHOLE ARMOR

Before playing, cut out the pieces and assemble the board game. Grab a die to play!

Objective: To put on the whole armor of God.

Instructions:
Roll the die and move that many spaces.

1. If you land on a blank space, stand up and do that many jumps to get wiggles out. For example, if you rolled a 3, do 3 jumps and then roll again.
2. If you land on a picture of Jesus, the parent offers two choices, good and bad. Help your child choose the good choice.
3. If you land on a music note, sing a primary song.
4. When you land on one of the armor pieces, stop; do not pass it! Read the scripture on the armor and let your child put that piece of armor on the paper doll. Explain in simple terms what that means. An excerpt in the June 2016 Friend that has great, simple explanations. Click/scan the link to find that article.

The Whole Armor of God

5. Keep playing until the paper doll is dressed in the whole armor of God!

PUT ON THE ARMOR

RMOR OF GOD GAME

D&C 27:18

D&C 27:18

D&C 27:15

D&C 27:16

D&C 27:15

D&C 27:15

D&C 27:15

Made in the USA
Columbia, SC
28 January 2025

52355346R10096